85 Differentiated Word Sorts

One-Page Leveled Word Sorts
for Building Decoding
& Spelling Skills

Janiel M. Wagstaff

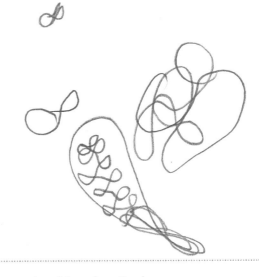

New York • Toronto • London • Auckland • Sydney
Mexico City • New Delhi • Hong Kong • Buenos Aires

DEDICATION

For those who work so hard to support growing readers and writers. My best to you!

ACKNOWLEDGMENTS

Thank you, Max, for giving up mom-time so other kids might benefit from this work. You really are "Miracle Max!" Thanks once again, Mom and Dad, for all you do to support us.

Scholastic Inc. grants teachers permission to photocopy the reproducible pages from this book for classroom use. Purchase of this book entitles use of reproducibles by one teacher for one classroom only. No other part of this publication may be reproduced in whole or in part, or stored in a retrieval system, or transmitted in any form or by any means, electronic, mechanical, photocopying, recording, or otherwise, without written permission of the publisher. For information regarding permission, write to Scholastic Inc., 557 Broadway, New York, NY 10012.

Editor: Maria L. Chang
Cover design by Tannaz Fassihi
Photos by Adam Chinitz
Interior design by Grafica Inc.

ISBN: 978-0-545-90736-1
Copyright © 2016 by Janiel Wagstaff
All rights reserved.
Printed in the U.S.A.
First printing, June 2016.

3 4 5 6 7 8 9 10   131   22 21 20 19

TABLE OF CONTENTS

Introduction 4

Short a
at,* am,* ack* 12
an,* ad, ap* 13
ant, ask, ag* 14
and, ab,* ank* 15

Short e
end, est,* ell* 16
en, et, ed* 17
ent, ep, em 18

Short i
ish, in,* iss 19
ift, ill,* im* 20
ick,* it, ip* 21
ing,* ink* 22

Short o
op,* ock,* ot* 23
oss, od, ob* 24
og, om 25

Short u
ub, uck,* ug* 26
unk,* um,* ut 27
ump,* un, ust 28

Mixed Short Vowels 29–35

Long a
ame,* ate,* ake* 36
ade, ay,* ace 37
ail,* ain,* ave 38
ale,* ape, ane 39

Long e
een, eed,* eep 40
eat,* ee, eam 41
ear, each, eer 42
-y, ea, eel 43
ie, e, e-e 44

Long i
ite, ine,* ive 45
ice,* ike, ight* 46
ide,* ind, -y* 47
ie, igh, i-e 48

Long o
o, old, ope 49
oke,* ole, one 50
ow,* o-e, oat 51
oa, oe 52

Long u
u-e, ue 53
u, ew 54

Mixed Long Vowels 55–60

Mixed Long & Short Vowels 61–65

r-Controlled Vowels
ar, ark, art 66
or,* ore,* orn 67
er, ir,* ur 68
air, are, ear 69

Diphthongs & Variant Vowels
oy, all, oi 70
ow, ou, aw* 71
out,* ook, own 72
ound, ew,* au 73
u-e, oo, ood 74

Mixed Vowels 75–81

Consonant Digraphs
sh, th 82
wh, ch 83
ph, wr 84
ng, ck 85

Beginning Blends
bl, cl, fl 86
br, cr, gr 87
st, sw, sp 88
sc, str, sn 89
gl, pl, sl 90
fr, tr, pr 91

Ending Blends
-nd, -mp, -st 92
-sk, -ld, -nt 93

Affixes
un-, re-, dis- 94
-s, -es, -ed 95
-ing, -ly 96

NOTE: Chunks with * are combined from two high-frequency chunks lists (Wylie & Durrell, 1970, and Fry, 1998).

INTRODUCTION

Most of us have been using word sorts to develop children's word recognition and spelling abilities in our classrooms for years. Why? Because they've been found to be such effective tools for helping children see, hear, and understand how spelling patterns work in words. When we look at the work of top spelling and phonics researchers in this area (Bear et al, 2016; Blevins, 2006, 2016; and others), sorts are always mentioned as one of the best ways to help children process and practice letter-sound patterns. If you've used sorts like I have, I'm sure you can vouch for the difference they make in helping children become automatic at recognizing phonics patterns while reading and using these patterns in their writing—which is, of course, the ultimate goal of our work with sorts.

But why do we need another book of word sorts? There can't possibly be anything new in this area, right? Think again! I wrote *85 Differentiated Word Sorts* to make our jobs as teachers easier. I've formatted the sorts so you get everything you need on one page—no need to find and copy multiple word sorts to meet children's diverse needs. **This books makes differentiating a snap!** On just one page you'll find words conveniently organized by differing levels of complexity using the same chunk (rime), vowel pattern, digraph, blend, or affix. Simply cut the page to give children exactly what they need based on their decoding/spelling abilities. (I'll explain how this works in detail using concrete examples in the pages ahead.)

Another key factor that makes these sorts valuable is that they include **ALL of the highest-frequency chunks or rimes** that make up a HUGE number of other words, as identified by research (Wylie & Durrell, 1970; Fry, 1998). Since these chunks make up hundreds of different one-syllable words, imagine their potential impact when we factor in all the multisyllabic words they make up. Obviously, automaticity with these chunks really pays off for our readers and spellers. When we augment instruction and practice with the use of Word Walls and teach children analogy strategies so they can use the word parts to read and write a host of other words, we do much to increase children's decoding proficiency while pushing their spelling development to higher levels (Wagstaff, 1994, 1999, 2009, 2011, 2016).

The sorts in this book are not limited to just the highest-frequency chunks. I've included a significant number of other common chunks, as well as vowel, letter, and word patterns **(totaling 170)** to help you build your students' word knowledge.

DIFFERENTIATION IN ACTION

A snip here, a snip there … here's how to differentiate the sorts to meet children's needs!

end	est	ell
rest	bend	tell
sell	west	send
mend	vest	well

The most emergent children get the first three rows to read and sort. If necessary, you could even limit their work to just the first two rows.

Your next group might be able to handle words with more complex beginning sounds (onsets) and simple suffixes. So you can give them the first six rows.

end	est	ell
rest	bend	tell
sell	west	send
mend	vest	well
nest	tend	bells
smell	chest	blends
swell	zesty	testing

More developed children could probably handle an increasing number of two-syllable words with a variety of affixes. The vocabulary is becoming more complex, as well. Thus, the top eight rows in this example may be a good fit.*

end	est	ell
rest	bend	tell
sell	west	send
mend	vest	well
nest	tend	bells
smell	chest	blends
swell	zesty	testing
rested	yelled	ended
tender	teller	smelly

Your most advanced group may be able to try all of the words.* The bottom rows feature multisyllabic examples with a variety of affixes and more complex vocabulary.

end	est	ell
rest	bend	tell
sell	west	send
mend	vest	well
nest	tend	bells
smell	chest	blends
swell	zesty	testing
rested	yelled	ended
tender	teller	smelly
yellow	slender	crested
blending	festival	mellow

end	est	ell
rested	yelled	ended
tender	teller	smelly
yellow	slender	crested
blending	festival	mellow

*When assigning the harder rows, you don't necessarily have to give students *all* the preceding rows. Simply make another cut to eliminate rows you don't want, but be sure children get the headers at the top. For example, for your advanced group, you might cut out the headers, then make a second cut, so they have only the last four rows to read and sort, rather than the whole page. *Voilà!* Here is their workload. (This is just another option. You decide what best fits your students' needs.)

Adapting for K–1

In one school where I taught, several of my entering first graders could handle entire pages of these sorts as we worked through an appropriate sequence of skills. (Even so, the vocabulary was tough, so I had to spend a bit more time on that.) In most schools, though, a whole page of sorts would be too challenging for entering first graders. Obviously, tackling the whole page for even our highest-achieving kindergartners would be too much as well (although, there are always exceptions!). This is an easy fix. As with the examples above, simply leave off the bottom rows and include only rows of words that are appropriate for your children. In K–1 then, your cuts may happen in different places to differentiate groups. Perhaps your most advanced kindergartners get the first five rows, and your most advanced first graders get the first seven rows.

PROCEDURES

You might be wondering how to respond when children notice the differing workload: "Teeeaaacher … Why does Jennifer have fewer words to sort than I do? It's not fair!" Deal with this right up front to squelch ongoing complaints. For example, I say, *"Everyone in our class has different needs because we're growing at varied rates as readers and writers. It's just like how our bodies grow—we each grow at different rates. I work hard to figure out what will help each one of you learn the very best. You end up with different words to work on to help* you *grow."*

I might also add, *"Normally, I welcome talking about what we're doing in class, how it's going, and what seems fair. But our word sorts and …* (add other pertinent examples from your class here) *are exceptions. So, let's all do our work and not worry about what anyone else is doing."* (In other words, after your explanation, this topic is off the table for discussion.)

Here are some ideas for making sorting as productive as possible.

Cutting the words before sorting

I model this quick and easy procedure several times until students have it down pat.

1. Cut across the first horizontal line so you have your headers. DO NOT worry about the scraps. Snip on the vertical lines to separate each header card.

2. Cut upward on the vertical lines starting at the bottom of your page. Now you have three (sometimes two) columns of words.

3. Turn each column sideways and quickly snip each word. DO NOT worry about the scraps!

NOTE: I tell children beforehand not to worry about the scraps, because some will waste an inordinate amount of time meticulously cutting. Remind them that this is not art class, it's phonics practice! (Ever notice how your weakest readers will try to find ways to avoid reading? Enforcing this procedure will help you eliminate that problem.)

Sorting the words

Have children place the header cards at the top of three (or two) columns on their desks or on the floor. They then mix up the words they've cut. They pick a word, read it aloud (see sidebar), and place it under the appropriate header card.

Doing a quick check and class debrief after sorting

When children finish sorting their words, they ask a buddy to do a "quick check." The buddy uses a pencil or other tool to point randomly to any word in the sort (five or six random words is sufficient). The child reads these words aloud. If he or she gets stuck, the child refers back to the header card for help figuring out the word. *I* do the quick check with students who are struggling the most so I can better support them.

Afterward, debrief with the whole class, asking what they noticed in the sort. Encourage children to talk about the patterns and how they work.

> **A HARD-AND-FAST RULE**
>
> This is another procedure I model repeatedly (and have volunteers model for the class). I tell my students: *"Before sorting a word into its proper column, you MUST read it out loud. No exceptions! If you get stuck, read the other words you've already sorted in the column with the same letter pattern. If you still need help, ask a peer, then reread the word three times before placing it."* I add that I will be doing random checks as they sort, so they really have to read the words aloud to be prepared.

Cleaning up and extending the learning

After the debrief, have children collect their words and put them in an envelope. Ask them to list the headers—the chunks, vowel patterns, digraphs, blends, or affixes—on the front.

The next day, have students sort the words again, but this time, have them do it in one minute. To prepare for this timed sort, have children empty their envelopes, place the headers, and make sure all the words are face-up, ready to sort, and … *go!* Children love the game-like feel of this activity, and it helps build automaticity (Blevins, 2016). At the end of one minute, ask them to count how many words they were able to sort. Then have them remix the words and time them again. Challenge them to beat the number of words they sorted the first time. (Note: If one minute isn't an appropriate amount of time for your students, adjust as necessary.)

Later, invite children to take their envelope home, where they resort and reread the words with a parent or older sibling. This person can sign the envelope so it can be returned to school for "extra credit."

What about the more challenging vocabulary?

When handing children a sort that contains unfamiliar vocabulary words, have them point to each of the challenging words, say the word, and listen as you give a quick definition and example. Though this is not complete vocabulary instruction, it is at least something. Our goal with the sorts is for children to recognize patterns across words, hear how the sound of the pattern is consistent, build knowledge of patterns through practice, and use that knowledge to decode and spell new words. However, feel free to expand on the vocabulary instruction, either in small groups or with the whole class.

ENSURING CHILDREN MAKE THE CONNECTION TO SPELLING

Many teachers use word sorts to increase children's automaticity with word patterns for decoding. But what about spelling? We get the most bang for our buck and save time when we ensure the work we do with sorts extends into encoding. In fact, our phonics instruction should seamlessly go along with our spelling instruction, focusing on the same words and patterns for both. This heightens children's abilities to learn and make connections. We can do much more than simply including the same words from our sorts on spelling tests. Here are several ways to ensure the spelling connection really happens.

Post one key word on a Word Wall to represent each pattern under study. For example, when working on the "et" pattern, you might post the word *pet* in kindergarten and first grade, or the word *basket* in second and third grade (underline *et* in the word). Since you'll work on "et" (along with other patterns) all week, add the key words to a permanent Word Wall. This way you can refer to practiced patterns all year long as you read *and* write analogous words. Every day, as I engage in writing with students, I also model and think aloud about using known patterns from the Wall to spell words in our writing. I direct children to use the Wall and explain *their* connections as they help the class spell in shared writing contexts. The sheer repetition built into an active Word Wall helps move word patterns to long-term memory. (For more details on posting and using words on a Word Wall, see Wagstaff, 1999, 2009, 2011, and 2016.)

Another highly efficacious technique is to schedule guided spelling practice (what I call "Challenge Words") a couple times a week, following this procedure:

- Hold up a Word Wall card showing the key word containing the pattern under study.
- Invite children to read the word aloud, say the sound of the chunk, vowel pattern, digraph, blend, or affix, then spell that word part.
- Give the class (or smaller group) a few analogous words using that word part to spell independently. Begin by giving easier words, then, if appropriate, increase complexity to make the lesson multi-leveled. For example, holding up the Word Wall card *pet*, you might say: *"We know the* 'et' *chunk, e-t. Use what you know to spell the word* jet." After children write the word on their papers, ask them to call out their attempts. Write a few of these on the board. Invite the class or group to examine the spellings together to determine if students used a logical letter for the beginning sound and properly spelled the "et" chunk. Indicate which attempts are logical, then finish by writing the correct spelling on the board. Say: *"So, if we know the word* pet, p-e-t, *then we can easily spell* jet, j-e-t." Depending on the grade and children's ability levels, you might then offer another single-syllable word, this time with a consonant blend, digraph, or an affix (such as *vets*). Or, you might continue with single-syllable words or offer a multisyllabic word, like *carpet*, and finally increase the difficulty to something like *blankets*.
- For each key word (remember, you're using just one key word per pattern), have children attempt to spell three or four analogous words. To keep the pace brisk, call for and examine students' different attempts on only one or two of the dictated words (as with *jet* above). Work with each key word should last only three or four minutes. Repeat this process with the other key spelling patterns that are being practiced each week. On Friday, add the key words to the Word Wall.

Another simple idea is to dictate a few sentences of appropriate lengths using words containing the patterns under study (Blevins, 2016). This way, children apply their knowledge in the context of writing connected text.

Yet another effective practice is to highlight students' use of the word patterns you're studying (or that are already posted on the Word Wall) in their everyday writing. Place writing samples under the document camera and celebrate logical spelling attempts! (For many more ways to practice and further infuse the use of the Word Wall and patterns under study into daily reading and writing, see Wagstaff 1999, 2009, and 2011.)

A few things you'll notice about the sorts

In some cases, I've included words that fit under two headers in the same sort. For example, in the at/am/ack sort, the word *attack* could logically be placed under either *at* or *ack*, so I would accept the word as correct in either column. Though decoding the word /at/ /tack/ is a misreading of the first vowel, children decoding it this way, who have the word in their lexicons, should be able to self-correct the pronunciation error. It's always fun when children discover a word that can be sorted in more than one column. I ask, *"Which column do you think it belongs in?"* then have them explain their reasoning to peers (who might counter with their own reasoning). Rich phonics talk ensues!

Another similar issue occurs in the ar/ark/art, or/ore/orn, and u-e/oo/ood sorts. Any of the words in the /ar/ark/art/ sort can be sorted under /ar/ since they all contain this letter combination. We don't want children to do this, so be sure to instruct them to sort only those words in which /ar/ occurs by itself (without the *k* or *t*) in the /ar/ column. Give them the same instructions for sorting the or/ore/orn and u-e/oo/ood words.

DECODING MULTISYLLABIC WORDS

In my first book, *Phonics That Work!* (1994), I argued for flexibility when teaching young children to chunk words to decode and encode, rather than bogging them down with syllabication rules. Based on more than twenty years of work with K–3 learners since that time, I still stand by this philosophy.* Children might break down unknown multisyllabic words in multiple ways to decode or spell them. For example, when reading the word *interview*, a child might see /in/ /ter/ /view/ and blend the chunks to read the word according to correct syllabication rules, or he might see /int/ /er/ /view/ and read it with a slightly different stress on the first syllable. Since our end goal is for children to simply read the words, we shouldn't get too hung up on whether or not they broke the words down according to correct rules of syllabication, especially in the primary grades. Indeed, the Common Core State Standards say children in third grade should simply "decode multisyllabic words," while "knowledge of syllabication patterns" isn't included as a word-recognition strategy until fourth grade (National Governors Association Center for Best Practices, Council of Chief State School Officers, 2010).

I mention this because, as I wrote the word sorts, I included some words that don't follow syllabication rules, such as *fantasy* in the /ant/ask/ag/ sort. Yes, one can correctly break the word into syllables to read /fan/ /ta/ /sy/, or as it fits into this sort, one could read it as /fant/ /as/ /y/. Again, though not broken down according to rules, once blended it's "close enough" and when read in context, one's prior knowledge should kick in to assist in correcting the pronunciation (assuming the word is in the child's vocabulary).

*The books I've written with a word-work focus, such as *Using Word Walls to Teach Reading and Writing* (1999) and *Using Name Walls to Teach Reading and Writing* (2009), detail the same approach.

REFERENCES

Bear, D. R., S. Templeton, S. Invernizzi, M., and Johnston, F. (2016). *Words Their Way: Word Study for Phonics, Vocabulary and Spellings Instruction (6th Edition).* Upper Saddle River, NJ: Pearson.

Blevins, W. (2016). *A Fresh Look at Phonics.* Thousand Oaks, CA: Corwin

Blevins, W. (2006). *Phonics from A to Z: A Practical Guide.* New York: Scholastic.

Fry, E. (1998). The most common phonograms. *The Reading Teacher*, 51, 620–622.

National Governors Association Center for Best Practices, Council of Chief State School Officers. (2010). *Common Core State Standards.* Washington D.C.

Wagstaff, J. M. (2016). *The Common Core Companion K–2 Booster Lessons: Elevating Instruction Day by Day.* Thousand Oaks, CA: Corwin.

Wagstaff, J. M. (2011). *Quick Start to Writing Workshop Success.* New York: Scholastic.

Wagstaff, J. M. (2009). *Using Name Walls to Teach Reading and Writing.* New York: Scholastic.

Wagstaff, J. M. (1999). *Teaching Reading and Writing with Word Walls.* New York: Scholastic.

Wagstaff, J. M. (1994). *Phonics That Work! New Strategies for the Reading/Writing Classroom.* New York: Scholastic.

Wylie, R. E., and Durrell, D. D. (1970). Teaching vowels through phonograms. *Elementary English*, 47, 787–791.

COMMON CORE CONNECTIONS

Word sorts fit into the Foundational Skills standards of the Common Core, specifically under Phonics and Word Recognition.

Phonics and Word Recognition Standard 3: Know and apply grade-level phonics and word analysis skills in decoding words.

The work can be extended to include the Language Standard related to spelling, as explained on page 8.
Language Standard 2: Demonstrate command of the conventions of … spelling when writing.

KINDERGARTEN
RF.K.3.a Demonstrate basic knowledge of one-to-one letter-sound correspondences.
RF.K.3.b Associate the long and short sounds with common spellings for the five major vowels.
RF.K.3.d Distinguish between similarly spelled words by identifying the sounds of the letters that differ.
L.K.2.d Spell simple words phonetically, drawing on knowledge of letter-sound relationships.

FIRST GRADE
RF.1.3.a Know the spelling-sound correspondences for common consonant digraphs.
RF.1.3.b Decode regularly spelled one-syllable words.
RF.1.3.c Know final -e and common vowel team conventions for long vowel sounds.
RF.1.3.e Decode two-syllable words following basic patterns by breaking the words into syllables.
RF.1.3.f Read words with inflectional endings.
L.1.2.d Use conventional spelling for words with common spelling patterns.
L.1.2.e Spell untaught words phonetically, drawing on phonemic awareness and spelling conventions.

SECOND GRADE
RF.2.3.a Distinguish long and short vowels when reading regularly spelled one-syllable words.
RF.2.3.b Know spelling-sound correspondences for additional common vowel teams.
RF.2.3.c Decode regularly spelled two-syllable words with long vowels.
RF.2.3.d Decode words with common prefixes and suffixes.
RF.2.3.e Identify words with inconsistent but common spelling-sound correspondences.
L.2.2.d Generalize learned spelling patterns when writing words.

THIRD GRADE
RF.3.3.a Identify and know the meaning of the most common prefixes and derivational suffixes.
RF.3.3.c Decode multisyllable words.
L.3.2.e Use conventional spelling for high-frequency and other studied words and for adding suffixes to base words.
L.3.2.f Use spelling patterns and generalizations in writing words.

© Copyright 2010 National Governors Association Center for Best Practices and Council of Chief State School Officers. All rights reserved.

The Word Sorts

Short a

Cut apart the words. Make three columns. Place the **bold** cards at the top. Pick a word. Read it aloud. Sort the word. Then check.

at	**am**	**ack**
Sam	cat	back
Jack	fat	ram
rat	pack	Pam
chat	tram	crack
hams	black	flat
stack	gram	chatted
splat	attack	tracks
scatter	cracker	mammal
backpack	shamrock	mattress
ambulance	acrobat	packets

Cut apart the words. Make three columns. Place the **bold** cards at the top. Pick a word. Read it aloud. Sort the word. Then check.

an	**ad**	**ap**
tap	ran	sad
fan	bad	sap
lad	nap	tan
lap	pans	Tad
Stan	fad	snap
Brad	wraps	apple
unwrap	badly	answer
sadder	handles	happier
snapping	gladden	granny
maddest	Japanese	transformer

Short a

Cut apart the words. Make three columns. Place the **bold** cards at the top. Pick a word. Read it aloud. Sort the word. Then check.

ant	**ask**	**ag**
bag	ants	ask
tag	mask	pant
rant	rag	task
sag	bask	baggy
masks	chant	drag
saggy	flask	slant
planted	asked	wagging
dragons	granting	masked
bagpipes	basketball	fantasy
wastebasket	antler	magazine

Cut apart the words. Make three columns. Place the **bold** cards at the top. Pick a word. Read it aloud. Sort the word. Then check.

Short a

and	**ab**	**ank**
dab	sand	tank
hand	tab	sank
lab	rank	land
slab	band	jab
stank	blank	brand
stand	habit	ankle
rabbit	grand	handy
standing	bankers	absent
grabby	blankets	handles
Anderson	fabulous	crankier

Short e

Cut apart the words. Make three columns. Place the **bold** cards at the top. Pick a word. Read it aloud. Sort the word. Then check.

end	**est**	**ell**
rest	bend	tell
sell	west	send
mend	vest	well
nest	tend	bells
smell	chest	blends
swell	zesty	testing
rested	yelled	ended
tender	teller	smelly
yellow	slender	crested
blending	festival	mellow

Cut apart the words. Make three columns. Place the **bold** cards at the top. Pick a word. Read it aloud. Sort the word. Then check.

Short e

en	**et**	**ed**
ten	pet	red
let	bed	hen
Ted	pen	set
den	wet	wed
when	fled	fret
sheds	forget	Jenny
basket	bedroom	edit
energy	blankets	regret
medicine	enlarge	bracelets
entrance	banquet	envelope

Short e — Cut apart the words. Make three columns. Place the **bold** cards at the top. Pick a word. Read it aloud. Sort the word. Then check.

ent	**ep**	**em**
hem	sent	pep
went	step	gem
them	gems	bent
wept	tent	memo
rent	lemon	slept
tremble	spent	pepper
footsteps	temple	absent
venting	assembly	overslept
peppermint	current	rental
represent	intercept	embarrass

Cut apart the words. Make three columns. Place the **bold** cards at the top. Pick a word. Read it aloud. Sort the word. Then check.

Short i

ish	**in**	**iss**
in	fish	kiss
miss	pin	dish
wish	tin	hiss
bins	fishy	wins
shin	bliss	swish
kisses	dishes	grin
winner	missing	inside
Trisha	thinnest	wishing
dismiss	polish	interest
incredible	blissful	cherished

19

Short i

Cut apart the words. Make three columns. Place the **bold** cards at the top. Pick a word. Read it aloud. Sort the word. Then check.

ift	**ill**	**im**
will	Jim	gift
hill	lift	rim
dim	Bill	rift
spill	drift	grim
swift	slim	still
chilly	shifts	swims
swimmer	fifty	illness
thrilling	trimming	airlift
brimming	forklift	timber
giftwrap	windowsill	important

Cut apart the words. Make three columns. Place the **bold** cards at the top. Pick a word. Read it aloud. Sort the word. Then check.

Short i

ick	it	ip
hip	sick	sit
sip	hit	lick
chick	bit	tip
chip	brick	fit
chicken	knit	clip
kitten	tricky	shipping
clipper	itself	stickers
flicker	flipped	written
slippers	quitter	lipstick
trickster	shipyards	bandits

Short i

Cut apart the words. Make two columns. Place the **bold** cards at the top. Pick a word. Read it aloud. Sort the word. Then check.

ing	**ink**
ink	sing
ding	sink
pink	wings
thing	mink
stink	sting
think	bring
singer	shrink
clingy	stringy
stinging	rethink
trinkets	draining

Cut apart the words. Make three columns. Place the **bold** cards at the top. Pick a word. Read it aloud. Sort the word. Then check.

Short o

op	**ock**	**ot**
pot	sock	pop
cop	hot	hop
rock	jot	lock
plot	chop	block
drop	clock	spot
socks	shots	blocks
knocked	mopping	spotted
jotting	pocket	hottest
unstopped	otter	lockers
shocking	pottery	chopping

Short o

Cut apart the words. Make three columns. Place the **bold** cards at the top. Pick a word. Read it aloud. Sort the word. Then check.

oss	**od**	**ob**
nod	boss	job
Bob	pod	toss
loss	cob	rod
rob	plod	moss
floss	pods	bossy
blob	across	snobby
glosses	knobs	body
slobber	model	flossing
clobber	robbers	nodded
remodeling	doorknobs	motocross

Cut apart the words. Make two columns. Place the **bold** cards at the top. Pick a word. Read it aloud. Sort the word. Then check.

Short o

og	**om**
dog	mom
Tom	fog
hog	jog
dogs	moms
prom	logs
clog	frogs
pom-pom	soggy
omelets	clogged
bullfrog	atomic
promise	groundhog

Short u

Cut apart the words. Make three columns. Place the **bold** cards at the top. Pick a word. Read it aloud. Sort the word. Then check.

ub	**uck**	**ug**
tuck	rub	rug
tug	duck	sub
dug	tub	luck
buck	rubs	mug
stuck	truck	chub
ugly	club	chuck
lucky	tubby	grub
buckets	struck	hugging
chugged	bubble	buckles
clucking	rugged	rubble

Cut apart the words. Make three columns. Place the **bold** cards at the top. Pick a word. Read it aloud. Sort the word. Then check.

Short u

unk	**um**	**ut**
bunk	but	hum
sum	sunk	hut
cut	chum	junk
crumb	rut	tummy
chunk	mummy	butter
lumber	stunk	flutter
stutter	humble	skunks
umbrella	chunky	shutters
butterfly	stumble	clunky
buttonholes	junkyard	summary

Short u

Cut apart the words. Make three columns. Place the **bold** cards at the top. Pick a word. Read it aloud. Sort the word. Then check.

ump	**un**	**ust**
just	fun	jump
run	bust	dump
bun	hump	must
trust	clump	sun
sunny	crust	stump
jumping	lumpy	rusty
under	trusted	plump
mustard	clumped	thunder
hundred	custards	grumpy
crumpets	understand	justify

Cut apart the words. Make three columns. Place the **bold** cards at the top. Pick a word. Read it aloud. Sort the word. Then check.

Mixed Short Vowels

an	**est**	**op**
pop	ran	rest
fan	west	cop
hop	vest	tan
nest	pans	tops
Stan	chest	stop
chops	zesty	plans
rested	hopping	answer
sloppy	handles	chopped
lollipop	crested	granny
transformer	festival	helicopter

29

Mixed Short Vowels

Cut apart the words. Make three columns. Place the **bold** cards at the top. Pick a word. Read it aloud. Sort the word. Then check.

uck	**ill**	**ank**
will	tuck	tank
duck	sank	hill
rank	Bill	luck
spill	buck	plank
truck	blank	still
stank	chilly	chuck
lucky	illness	ankles
thrilling	bankers	struck
blankets	buckles	grilled
windowsill	clucking	crankier

Cut apart the words. Make three columns. Place the **bold** cards at the top. Pick a word. Read it aloud. Sort the word. Then check.

Mixed Short Vowels

ock	**at**	**ell**
cat	sock	tell
sell	fat	lock
socks	well	rat
bells	chat	clock
block	smell	flat
chats	blocked	swell
yelled	splat	knocked
chatter	teller	pocket
lockers	mattress	yellow
mellow	shocking	acrobats

31

Mixed Short Vowels

Cut apart the words. Make three columns. Place the **bold** cards at the top. Pick a word. Read it aloud. Sort the word. Then check.

ack	**ip**	**unk**
hip	back	bunk
Jack	sunk	sip
junk	pack	tip
lip	chunk	crack
stunk	black	chip
stack	drips	trunk
skunks	shipping	attack
clipper	crackers	chunky
backpack	lipstick	clunky
shipyards	junkyard	packets

Cut apart the words. Make three columns. Place the **bold** cards at the top.
Pick a word. Read it aloud. Sort the word. Then check.

Mixed Short Vowels

ob	**ick**	**ap**
sick	job	tap
Bob	sap	lick
nap	chick	cob
brick	lap	rob
blob	chicken	snap
apple	knob	tricky
sticky	trapped	robber
slobber	flicker	happier
snapping	corncob	stickers
trickster	Japanese	clobbered

Mixed Short Vowels

Cut apart the words. Make three columns. Place the **bold** cards at the top. Pick a word. Read it aloud. Sort the word. Then check.

um	**ag**	**it**
hum	bag	sit
tag	hit	sum
bum	rag	bit
fit	chum	sag
drag	knit	crumb
kitten	saggy	tummy
mummy	itself	wagging
lumber	bagpipes	written
dragons	quitter	humble
umbrellas	magazines	bandits

Cut apart the words. Make three columns. Place the **bold** cards at the top. Pick a word. Read it aloud. Sort the word. Then check.

Mixed Short Vowels

am	**ed**	**in**
in	Sam	red
ram	bed	pin
Ted	tin	Pam
bins	tram	wed
hams	fled	shin
sheds	gram	grin
winner	bedroom	inside
fretted	interest	mammal
medicine	shamrock	thinnest
ambulance	incredible	educate

Long a

Cut apart the words. Make three columns. Place the **bold** cards at the top. Pick a word. Read it aloud. Sort the word. Then check.

ame	**ate**	**ake**
hate	make	game
take	late	same
name	rake	mate
gate	lame	fake
blame	rates	Blake
later	awake	grate
tamed	dated	mistake
plates	became	skated
mistaken	framed	states
milkshakes	update	ashamed

36

Cut apart the words. Make three columns. Place the **bold** cards at the top. Pick a word. Read it aloud. Sort the word. Then check.

Long a

ade	**ay**	**ace**
day	made	face
fade	lace	say
race	hay	wade
blades	May	grace
play	trader	space
tray	shades	stray
braces	players	remade
parade	invade	mayor
crayons	arcade	misplace
daydream	lemonade	everyplace

Long a — Cut apart the words. Make three columns. Place the **bold** cards at the top. Pick a word. Read it aloud. Sort the word. Then check.

ail	**ain**	**ave**
nail	gave	pain
sail	rain	pail
save	rail	gain
rave	wave	tail
fail	pave	grain
brave	stain	snails
trains	rainy	mailed
graves	hailing	stained
brainy	shaved	trailer
sailors	complain	caveman

Cut apart the words. Make three columns. Place the **bold** cards at the top. Pick a word. Read it aloud. Sort the word. Then check.

Long a

ale	**ape**	**ane**
ape	cane	sale
Jane	male	cape
tape	lane	tale
pale	gape	mane
sane	tales	taped
stale	grape	planes
shape	crane	inhale
humane	female	scraped
scrapers	airplanes	exhale
nightingale	shapeless	seascape

Long e

Cut apart the words. Make three columns. Place the **bold** cards at the top. Pick a word. Read it aloud. Sort the word. Then check.

een	**eed**	**eep**
beep	seen	need
teen	deep	weed
feed	keen	weep
queen	sheep	seed
speed	green	sweep
screen	bleed	greed
deeper	unseen	indeed
needed	between	sleeping
seedling	creepy	fifteen
evergreen	steepest	disagreed

Cut apart the words. Make three columns. Place the **bold** cards at the top. Pick a word. Read it aloud. Sort the word. Then check.

Long e

eat	**ee**	**eam**
eat	beam	bee
tree	beat	seam
team	knee	heat
seat	flee	glee
cream	bleat	free
wheat	stream	seated
spree	cheated	creamy
dreaming	degree	eaten
meatloaf	disagree	moonbeam
heartbeat	upstream	carefree

Long e

Cut apart the words. Make three columns. Place the **bold** cards at the top. Pick a word. Read it aloud. Sort the word. Then check.

ear	**each**	**eer**
each	deer	dear
jeer	year	peach
tear	beach	ears
reach	peer	gear
teach	clear	bleach
shear	preach	sneer
steers	beaches	hearing
career	speared	teaching
earring	cheerful	eerie
fearlessly	bleachers	engineer

Cut apart the words. Make three columns. Place the **bold** cards at the top. Pick a word. Read it aloud. Sort the word. Then check.

Long e

-y	**ea**	**eel**
peel	baby	pea
lady	sea	feel
tea	eels	happy
reel	tiny	ear
windy	seal	funny
leaf	steel	dirty
sneak	Ricky	wheels
kneel	witty	steam
gritty	leave	feelings
sweaty	cartwheel	teapots

43

Long e

Cut apart the words. Make three columns. Place the **bold** cards at the top. Pick a word. Read it aloud. Sort the word. Then check.

ie	e	e-e
he	eve	field
yield	brief	be
me	Pete	piece
Steve	shield	she
cookie	Peter	ego
movie	these	belief
egret	Steven	auntie
theme	sweetie	equal
Egypt	delete	genie
concrete	smoothie	evening

Cut apart the words. Make three columns. Place the **bold** cards at the top. Pick a word. Read it aloud. Sort the word. Then check.

Long i

ite	**ine**	**ive**
fine	bite	dive
kite	hive	dine
jive	site	mine
bites	nine	live
drive	lined	write
spines	hives	white
quite	twine	spite
recline	alive	unite
defined	rewrite	drivers
strives	valentine	graphite

Long i

Cut apart the words. Make three columns. Place the **bold** cards at the top. Pick a word. Read it aloud. Sort the word. Then check.

ice	**ike**	**ight**
tight	rice	bike
mice	might	Mike
hike	dice	nice
price	right	alike
hiker	twice	sight
lightly	trike	slices
nicest	flights	strikes
dislike	priced	brighten
delighted	likeness	devices
sacrifice	childlike	airtight

Cut apart the words. Make three columns. Place the **bold** cards at the top.
Pick a word. Read it aloud. Sort the word. Then check.

Long i

ide	**ind**	**-y**
ride	my	find
mind	side	by
sky	kind	wide
blind	tide	fly
slide	behind	why
myself	rider	binder
blinded	inside	crying
outside	frying	widen
stride	trying	rewind
reminders	nationwide	plywood

Long i

Cut apart the words. Make three columns. Place the **bold** cards at the top. Pick a word. Read it aloud. Sort the word. Then check.

ie	**igh**	**i-e**
die	pie	high
sigh	hive	lie
tie	sighs	ride
side	lies	tight
skies	bite	thigh
higher	dried	glide
sighed	fried	alive
untied	awhile	tonight
inside	magpie	uptight
alright	guidelines	necktie

Cut apart the words. Make three columns. Place the **bold** cards at the top. Pick a word. Read it aloud. Sort the word. Then check.

Long o

o	**old**	**ope**
hope	go	old
no	bold	rope
hold	nope	so
cope	Flo	sold
cold	gold	hero
hoped	fold	slopes
yo-yo	older	scope
coldest	going	hopeful
hopeless	golden	obeyed
blindfold	overload	telescope

Long o

Cut apart the words. Make three columns. Place the **bold** cards at the top. Pick a word. Read it aloud. Sort the word. Then check.

oke	**ole**	**one**
hole	cone	joke
tone	woke	mole
yoke	pole	bone
zone	sole	poke
awoke	alone	token
smoke	stolen	phone
stones	broken	rezone
resole	boneless	stroked
jokesters	cheekbone	buttonhole
artichoke	console	birthstone

Cut apart the words. Make three columns. Place the **bold** cards at the top. Pick a word. Read it aloud. Sort the word. Then check.

Long o

ow	**o-e**	**oat**
robe	row	oat
blow	boat	rode
coat	crow	home
rope	goat	grow
moat	show	tote
flows	float	wrote
frozen	throats	lower
snowy	towing	rowboats
mower	oatmeal	lonesome
homemaker	slowest	raincoats

Long o

Cut apart the words. Make two columns. Place the **bold** cards at the top. Pick a word. Read it aloud. Sort the word. Then check.

oa	**oe**
Joe	soap
doe	moan
loan	road
hoe	load
soapy	toes
toads	loaning
upload	tiptoe
tiptoed	railroad
goalpost	mistletoe
charcoals	uploading

Cut apart the words. Make two columns. Place the **bold** cards at the top. Pick a word. Read it aloud. Sort the word. Then check.

Long u

u-e	**ue**
use	cue
cute	hue
huge	cube
mute	mule
fuse	fuel
fumes	value
fuels	cured
argue	refuse
rescue	excuse
computers	continue

Long u

Cut apart the words. Make two columns. Place the **bold** cards at the top. Pick a word. Read it aloud. Sort the word. Then check.

u	**ew**
few	Utah
emu	mew
pew	unit
music	pews
fewer	human
museum	fewest
review	unicorn
utensil	curfew
nephew	unicycle
ukulele	interview

Cut apart the words. Make three columns. Place the **bold** cards at the top. Pick a word. Read it aloud. Sort the word. Then check.

Mixed Long Vowels

ail	**eed**	**-y**
my	nail	need
sail	weed	by
feed	sky	rail
tail	seed	fly
speed	fail	shy
myself	greed	snails
mailed	indeed	crying
needed	hailing	frying
greedy	trying	trailer
plywood	sailors	seedlings

55

Mixed Long Vowels

Cut apart the words. Make three columns. Place the **bold** cards at the top. Pick a word. Read it aloud. Sort the word. Then check.

ake	**-y**	**ight**
make	baby	tight
lady	take	might
right	happy	rake
fake	sight	bright
flight	Blake	windy
dirty	awake	lightly
shaken	Ricky	flights
witty	brighten	mistake
delighted	mistaken	gritty
milkshakes	sweaty	nightmare

Cut apart the words. Make three columns. Place the **bold** cards at the top. Pick a word. Read it aloud. Sort the word. Then check.

Mixed Long Vowels

oat	**ine**	**ay**
oat	day	fine
boat	dine	say
hay	coat	mine
nine	May	goat
play	moat	lined
float	spines	stray
throats	players	twine
mayor	recline	rowboats
defined	oatmeal	crayons
daydreams	valentines	raincoats

Mixed Long Vowels

Cut apart the words. Make three columns. Place the **bold** cards at the top. Pick a word. Read it aloud. Sort the word. Then check.

ew	**ind**	**eam**
find	few	beam
pew	seam	mind
team	kind	pews
blind	ream	rind
teams	behind	cream
stream	fewest	binder
blinded	creamy	review
steaming	curfew	kindest
nephew	rewind	daydream
interview	upstream	reminders

Cut apart the words. Make three columns. Place the **bold** cards at the top. Pick a word. Read it aloud. Sort the word. Then check.

Mixed Long Vowels

ope	**eat**	**ade**
hope	made	eat
fade	beat	rope
nope	wade	heat
blades	seat	cope
bleat	trader	slope
slopes	seated	shades
remade	scope	cheated
eaten	invade	hoped
hopeless	meatloaf	arcade
lemonade	telescopes	heartbeat

Mixed Long Vowels

Cut apart the words. Make three columns. Place the **bold** cards at the top. Pick a word. Read it aloud. Sort the word. Then check.

one	**ear**	**ate**
cone	hate	dear
tone	year	late
mate	bone	tear
gear	gate	zone
rates	clear	alone
hearing	phone	grate
stones	dated	shear
plates	speared	boneless
earrings	cheekbone	states
fearlessly	updated	birthstone

Cut apart the words. Make three columns. Place the **bold** cards at the top. Pick a word. Read it aloud. Sort the word. Then check.

Mixed Short & Long Vowels

et	**oke**	**u-e**
joke	use	pet
let	woke	cute
huge	set	yoke
wet	poke	cube
token	fumes	fret
forget	cuter	smoke
broken	basket	refuse
amuse	stroked	blankets
bracelets	excused	jokesters
artichoke	banquet	computers

Mixed Short & Long Vowels

Cut apart the words. Make three columns. Place the **bold** cards at the top. Pick a word. Read it aloud. Sort the word. Then check.

i-e	**ab**	**oa**
dab	hide	coal
moan	tab	side
hive	road	lab
jab	bite	load
white	soapy	slabs
toads	habit	alive
rabbit	awhile	loaning
slides	uploads	absent
railroad	grabby	outside
fabulous	goalpost	guidelines

Cut apart the words. Make three columns. Place the **bold** cards at the top. Pick a word. Read it aloud. Sort the word. Then check.

Mixed Short & Long Vowels

ain	**ea**	**ish**
fish	pea	pain
sea	rain	dish
gain	wish	tea
fishy	ear	pains
seals	grain	swish
stain	dishes	leaf
teach	sneak	rainy
Trisha	stained	teacher
beaches	polish	brainy
chaining	teapots	cherished

Mixed Short & Long Vowels

Cut apart the words. Make three columns. Place the **bold** cards at the top. Pick a word. Read it aloud. Sort the word. Then check.

oss	**ame**	**ike**
boss	game	bike
same	Mike	toss
hike	loss	name
moss	lame	alike
blame	bossy	hiker
trike	tamed	across
glossy	strikes	became
disliked	crossing	framed
flossing	ashamed	likeness
inflamed	childlike	motocross

64

Cut apart the words. Make three columns. Place the **bold** cards at the top.
Pick a word. Read it aloud. Sort the word. Then check.

Mixed Short & Long Vowels

ee	**un**	**ace**
face	bee	fun
run	lace	see
tree	bun	race
grace	feed	sun
sunny	space	seed
speed	laces	funny
braces	under	spree
thunder	agree	traced
creepy	misplaced	hundred
understand	disagree	everyplace

r-Controlled Vowels

Cut apart the words. Make three columns. Place the **bold** cards at the top. Pick a word. Read it aloud. Sort the word. Then check.

ar	**ark**	**art**
bark	part	car
tar	park	tart
bar	mart	dark
lark	shark	carts
spark	chart	hard
smart	harp	stark
guitar	barked	starting
partner	parking	costars
artistic	carpool	charcoal
markers	cartwheel	handlebar

66

Cut apart the words. Make three columns. Place the **bold** cards at the top. Pick a word. Read it aloud. Sort the word. Then check.

r-Controlled Vowels

or	**ore**	**orn**
corn	or	bore
for	born	core
torn	tore	horn
more	worn	cord
forks	store	porch
before	adore	order
afford	corner	adorn
bookstore	thorny	landlord
airport	boredom	unicorn
mornings	reordered	explorers

r-Controlled Vowels

Cut apart the words. Make three columns. Place the **bold** cards at the top. Pick a word. Read it aloud. Sort the word. Then check.

er	**ir**	**ur**
her	sir	curl
stir	burn	verb
germ	dirt	hurt
birds	term	curb
third	churn	ferns
purse	stern	shirts
skirts	nurse	nerve
squirted	clerks	churning
blurted	birthday	merge
quirky	suburbs	swerved

Cut apart the words. Make three columns. Place the **bold** cards at the top.
Pick a word. Read it aloud. Sort the word. Then check.

r-Controlled Vowels

air	**are**	**ear**
bear	air	care
dare	pear	fair
hair	hare	wear
rare	lair	pair
chair	swear	scare
wears	flair	share
hairy	glare	square
wearing	unfair	aware
upstairs	stared	careful
barefooted	airports	sleepwear

69

Diphthongs & Variant Vowels

Cut apart the words. Make three columns. Place the **bold** cards at the top. Pick a word. Read it aloud. Sort the word. Then check.

oy	**all**	**oi**
oil	toy	tall
call	boil	boy
joy	ball	soil
coil	boys	fall
halls	spoil	ahoy
noise	small	oinks
enjoyed	moist	tallest
spoiled	stalling	annoy
employ	pointers	enthrall
basketballs	avoided	employees

Cut apart the words. Make three columns. Place the **bold** cards at the top.
Pick a word. Read it aloud. Sort the word. Then check.

Diphthongs & Variant Vowels

ow	**ou**	**aw**
now	saw	our
ouch	cow	paw
raw	wow	loud
noun	draw	how
chow	couch	power
straws	flower	mouth
houses	awful	shower
chowder	towel	loudest
hourglass	eyebrow	flawless
empowers	jawbreaker	recounted

Diphthongs & Variant Vowels

Cut apart the words. Make three columns. Place the **bold** cards at the top. Pick a word. Read it aloud. Sort the word. Then check.

out	**ook**	**own**
book	out	down
pout	took	gown
cook	towns	about
brown	brook	nook
shout	crook	clown
trout	unhook	frowned
drowning	bookmark	spout
grout	snouts	cooking
outside	nightgown	crooked
meltdown	overlooked	reroute

Cut apart the words. Make three columns. Place the **bold** cards at the top. Pick a word. Read it aloud. Sort the word. Then check.

ound	**ew**	**au**
new	hound	auto
autos	dew	mound
bound	haul	blew
crew	found	cause
pause	grew	pound
vault	around	newer
sounded	stewed	haunt
taunt	chewing	flounder
haunted	grounded	redrew
playground	unscrew	background

Cut apart the words. Make three columns. Place the **bold** cards at the top. Pick a word. Read it aloud. Sort the word. Then check.

Diphthongs & Variant Vowels

u-e	**oo**	**ood**
boo	rude	good
tune	wood	too
hood	moo	rule
zoo	June	woods
flute	stood	shoot
drool	prune	goody
wooden	reboot	rudely
zooming	salute	hoodie
adulthood	shampoo	conclude
attitude	likelihood	foolishness

Cut apart the words. Make three columns. Place the **bold** cards at the top. Pick a word. Read it aloud. Sort the word. Then check.

Mixed Vowels

eep	**ore**	**ut**
beep	bore	but
core	hut	deep
cut	weep	sore
sheep	more	rut
butter	store	sweep
shores	flutter	before
stutter	deeper	adore
sleeping	bookstore	shutters
butterfly	creepy	boredom
explorers	buttonholes	steepest

Cut apart the words. Make three columns. Place the **bold** cards at the top. Pick a word. Read it aloud. Sort the word. Then check.

ir	**end**	**ow**
sir	bend	row
blow	stir	send
mend	crow	dirt
grow	tend	birds
third	show	blends
shirts	ended	flow
tender	lower	skirts
towing	attend	squirted
birthdays	mower	slender
blending	quirky	slowest

Cut apart the words. Make three columns. Place the **bold** cards at the top. Pick a word. Read it aloud. Sort the word. Then check.

Mixed Vowels

oy	**iss**	**air**
air	kiss	toy
miss	hair	boy
fair	joy	hiss
boys	misses	chair
bliss	paired	ahoy
hairy	enjoys	kisses
missing	dairy	enjoyed
airport	annoy	blissful
employ	dismiss	airfares
chairmen	employee	crisscross

77

Mixed Vowels

Cut apart the words. Make three columns. Place the **bold** cards at the top. Pick a word. Read it aloud. Sort the word. Then check.

ink	**oo**	**ad**
ink	sad	boo
bad	goo	sink
boot	pink	lad
Tad	mink	pool
roots	fad	stinks
think	hooted	Brad
igloo	badly	shrink
sadder	blinked	cuckoo
yahoo	gladden	rethink
trinkets	shampoo	maddest

78

Cut apart the words. Make three columns. Place the **bold** cards at the top. Pick a word. Read it aloud. Sort the word. Then check.

Mixed Vowels

and	**ar**	**eel**
car	sand	peel
hand	feel	tar
eels	bar	land
hard	band	reel
steel	carts	brand
stand	wheels	guitar
costars	grand	feelings
standing	kneeled	carpool
starring	artists	handles
grandstand	cartwheel	handlebar

Mixed Vowels

Cut apart the words. Make three columns. Place the **bold** cards at the top. Pick a word. Read it aloud. Sort the word. Then check.

ook	**ub**	**igh**
book	rub	high
sub	sigh	took
sighs	cook	tub
rubs	tight	brook
thigh	crook	chub
unhook	club	higher
tubby	tonight	bookmark
sighed	crooked	rubbed
uptight	bubble	unhooking
rubble	overlooked	nearsighted

Cut apart the words. Make three columns. Place the **bold** cards at the top. Pick a word. Read it aloud. Sort the word. Then check.

Mixed Vowels

er	**own**	**au**
auto	her	down
verb	gown	autos
haul	towns	germ
terms	cause	brown
clown	ferns	pause
vault	frowned	stern
nerve	haunt	drowning
brownish	clerks	taunt
haunted	nightgown	merge
meltdown	vaulted	swerved

Cut apart the words. Make two columns. Place the **bold** cards at the top. Pick a word. Read it aloud. Sort the word. Then check.

sh	**th**
thin	ship
thing	shut
shop	thug
think	shin
shake	thick
shine	thanks
three	sheet
shadow	third
thirsty	shelter
shampoo	Thursday

Cut apart the words. Make two columns. Place the **bold** cards at the top. Pick a word. Read it aloud. Sort the word. Then check.

Consonant Digraphs

wh	**ch**
chip	what
why	chin
chop	when
champ	whim
wham	chase
chain	wheels
whale	cheap
wheat	chores
whistle	channel
chipmunk	whimpered

Consonant Digraphs

Cut apart the words. Make two columns. Place the **bold** cards at the top. Pick a word. Read it aloud. Sort the word. Then check.

ph	**wr**
phone	wrap
wren	photo
graph	wrist
Ralph	wreck
wrath	phase
wrong	gopher
dolphins	written
wrinkle	sphere
wrestlers	alphabet
photograph	shipwreck

Cut apart the words. Make two columns. Place the **bold** cards at the top. Pick a word. Read it aloud. Sort the word. Then check.

Consonant Digraphs

ng	**ck**
tack	long
tick	sang
rung	rack
yuck	fangs
flung	block
sticks	strong
lucky	hanger
longest	uncheck
restock	English
wingspan	brackets

Cut apart the words. Make three columns. Place the **bold** cards at the top. Pick a word. Read it aloud. Sort the word. Then check.

bl	**cl**	**fl**
clam	blab	flag
flap	clap	blip
blob	clog	flip
flash	bless	cliff
clomp	flush	blink
flame	clean	bleed
clear	blame	fleet
blinds	flight	cloak
flowers	blizzard	cleaning
climate	flashlight	blossom

Cut apart the words. Make three columns. Place the **bold** cards at the top. Pick a word. Read it aloud. Sort the word. Then check.

Beginning Blends

br	**cr**	**gr**
crab	grin	brat
bran	crib	grub
grit	brick	crop
crack	grill	bring
brake	creep	green
grade	broke	croak
greedy	crown	brains
crunch	growl	breeze
brother	crayons	gravity
grandma	brightest	crickets

Beginning Blends

Cut apart the words. Make three columns. Place the **bold** cards at the top. Pick a word. Read it aloud. Sort the word. Then check.

st	**sw**	**sp**
swam	spin	star
stem	spot	swim
spit	swell	stop
swish	stack	spell
space	sweet	stone
sweep	speed	steal
steaks	swoop	speak
sport	steamed	swarm
swerve	speaker	stocking
starlight	speeches	swallow

Cut apart the words. Make three columns. Place the **bold** cards at the top. Pick a word. Read it aloud. Sort the word. Then check.

sc	**str**	**sn**
snap	strap	scab
strip	scat	snag
scan	snip	strut
snob	scuff	straw
stroll	sniff	scale
scare	strike	snake
sneak	scope	stripe
stream	sneeze	scarf
scooping	struggle	snatching
stretcher	scooters	snowplow

Beginning Blends

Cut apart the words. Make three columns. Place the **bold** cards at the top. Pick a word. Read it aloud. Sort the word. Then check.

gl	**pl**	**sl**
plan	sled	glop
slob	glob	plum
glad	plug	slip
plush	slush	glass
slant	glue	plow
glide	plays	slight
placed	sleepy	glee
sloped	glance	plain
slender	planet	glitter
plummet	glorious	slowpokes

Cut apart the words. Make three columns. Place the **bold** cards at the top. Pick a word. Read it aloud. Sort the word. Then check.

Beginning Blends

fr	**tr**	**pr**
trap	prod	frog
prop	frizz	trip
frill	press	trot
print	trash	fresh
tray	free	prize
frames	price	trace
prune	fright	treated
trailing	prance	frozen
Fridays	trumpet	problems
trample	princess	friendly

Ending Blends

Cut apart the words. Make three columns. Place the **bold** cards at the top. Pick a word. Read it aloud. Sort the word. Then check.

-nd	**-mp**	**-st**
best	and	lamp
bump	past	end
sand	lost	jump
dust	wind	fist
plump	blast	grand
east	blind	champ
stomp	ghost	found
ground	shrimp	toast
repump	rebound	distrust
streetlamp	breakfast	newsstand

Cut apart the words. Make three columns. Place the **bold** cards at the top. Pick a word. Read it aloud. Sort the word. Then check.

-sk	**-ld**	**-nt**
ant	ask	old
told	bent	desk
task	sold	hunt
held	mint	risk
brisk	scold	plant
paint	whisk	build
child	faint	unmask
kiosk	world	meant
absent	newsdesk	withheld
asterisk	pleasant	outfield

Affixes

Cut apart the words. Make three columns. Place the **bold** cards at the top. Pick a word. Read it aloud. Sort the word. Then check.

un-	**re-**	**dis-**
dislike	undo	redo
disobey	retell	unfair
refill	unlike	dismay
disable	unreal	rerun
repay	disagree	unhappy
remake	undress	distrust
unable	reload	dishonest
remove	disapprove	uncommon
rewrite	unhelpful	disconnect
disappears	replaced	unselfish

Cut apart the words. Make three columns. Place the **bold** cards at the top. Pick a word. Read it aloud. Sort the word. Then check.

Affixes

-s	-es	-ed
cats	liked	kisses
foxes	dogs	hiked
wishes	talked	kids
kicked	hills	boxes
dishes	birds	kissed
desks	bunches	pulled
chopped	sharks	brushes
classes	pitches	burgers
churches	puppets	shopped
replayed	flowers	flashes

Cut apart the words. Make two columns. Place the **bold** cards at the top. Pick a word. Read it aloud. Sort the word. Then check.

-ing	**-ly**
singing	slowly
badly	crying
sadly	fixing
getting	running
freely	gladly
kindly	bringing
shouting	safely
quickly	stringing
throwing	friendly
unfriendly	draining